Jump S Credit:

How to Negotiate and Settle your Debts in 10 Steps

You are one book away from better Credit and Financial Freedom !

To your Financial Success,

Leslie B Phillips

Jump Start Your Credit:
How to Negotiate and Settle your Debts in 10 Steps

Jump Start Your Credit:

How to Negotiate and Settle your Debts in 10 Steps

Lorillia Brown-Phillips

Prosperity Publishing

Published by
Prosperity Publishing
Bedminster, NJ

If you find typographical errors in this book they are here for a purpose. Some people actually enjoy looking for them and I strive to please as many people as possible.

Jump Start Your Credit:
How to Negotiate and Settle your Debts in 10 Steps

Legal Disclaimer:

Disclaimer: This book is designed to provide competent and reliable information
regarding the subject matter covered. However, it is sold with the understanding that the
author is not engaged in rendering legal, financial or other professional advice. Laws and
practices often vary from state to state and if legal or other expert assistance is required,
the services of a professional should be sought. The author specifically disclaim any
liability that is incurred from the use or application of the contents of this book.

Printed in the United State of America

Acknowledgements

To my husband Tommy and children Jaden & Aniya.
Thanks for your patient and support during those nights I
stayed up late and weekends I was away from home.

To the many talented professionals in the field of Financial
Literacy, who have not been published, the world is waiting
on your gift.
Life is too short, don't procrastinate get going. There is a
book in all of us!

Jump Start Your Credit:
How to Negotiate and Settle your Debts in 10 Steps

My $47 Dollar Gift for you!

First I want to thank you for buying this book, I want to give you a gift valued at $47 that is going to expand you knowledge in the area of rebuilding your credit and fighting debt collectors. Once you read this book you are going to be armed with so much knowledge, that you are going to be information overload. So I want to continue our dialogue, together going forward.

If you go to my website http://www.jumpstartyourcreditbook.com/freegift at the bottom of the website, and put in your email address I can send you a FREE GIFT. This is gift an audio valued at $47 dollars, the title of the audio is "**You Got Served! What to do if you're being sued by a Debt Collector**".

You have to go to the website to get the FREE GIFT.

The gift is yours with no strings attached. If you ever get tired of me sending you information (which I hope NEVER happens), all you have to do is click the UNSUBSCRIBE button that comes with every email that I send out. I know you already get tons of emails and you hate most of them. This will not be the case with the information that I will send you. You'll get a series of great take a ways that will help you prosper financially, and rebuild your credit. The information is something that you can put to use immediately. Do what it says on the website at the bottom the page. Go to http://www.jumpstartyourcreditbook.com/freegift.

Jump Start Your Credit:
How to Negotiate and Settle your Debts in 10 Steps

Preface

What motivated me to write this book on rebuilding your personal credit, when there are so many other books written on the subject, already on the market? Well for the reader who feels like there is no hope when it comes to getting rid of debt collectors and repairing your credit, I was just like you back in 1999.

In 1999, I had received a notice from my bank that a debt collector had levied my bank account for money they said I owed them. If you're not sure what levy means, well they took the money out of my bank account, no questions asked. The amount they took was roughly S2,200 dollars. This amount may not be a lot for some people but for me I felt violated and hopeless. My feelings at the moment were how could someone or a company just go right into my bank account and take my money without contacting me first. Well little did I know, they did contact me but I ignored their calls and their letters. Back in 1999, I did not know that there were laws that could protect people like me that owe debt collectors. I also did not know that there are Federal and State laws that debt collectors must follow when they are pursuing a debt from a consumer.

During my journey of discovering that what they did to me was wrong legally I did not want it to happen again. So I started my crusade to find out how I could prevent this from happening to me again.

There are so many books on rebuilding your credit, but there not a lot of books on how to fight debt collectors and negotiate your debts. When a debt collector contacts a consumer they are telling you that you have an outstanding debt that is not paid. Did you notice I said "they are telling you" and not "this is what about learning the difference with what a debt collectors say you owe and how it's being reported on your credit report. Incorrect information being reported on your credit report from a debt collector can ruin your chances of rebuilding your credit.

When it comes to dealing with a debt collector, there are not many books that will go into the necessary steps that one should follow when dealing with debt collectors. There are also no books that can explain to you the appropriate steps to take when, you try to negotiate with debt collectors to remove derogatory information off of your credit report. When I was faced with bad credit and constant harassment I thought the only solution is to pay those debts off, and I follow the advice from a credit repair book, which was and is all wrong. Paying off debts to a debt collector will only benefit the debt collector; it does not help increase your credit score. Many people do not know this.

If you really want to rebuild your credit or want debt collectors to stop harassing you it's important to learn the appropriate steps. Before you decide to pay any unpaid debts that are listed on your credit report, you must learn your rights. Financial ignorance is a billion dollar industry and debt collector are banking on the fact that you do not know the law, and a consumer who does not know the law will fall prey to a debt collector's tactics of bullying, threats and lawsuits. Remember before you decide to make the decision to rebuild your credit, learn the law before agreeing to make any payment that supposedly they say you "owe". I will go into this topic later in the book.

Introduction

Congratulations for taking the first step in eliminating your debt and improving your credit, it takes a brave person to face their financial situation and begin the process to improve their credit. Before you begin your journey with improving your credit you have to be honest with yourself, and ask the question. How did you get in this position in the first place?

By beginning to ask yourself that question, you can take notice of the situation and go forward with rebuilding your credit. This book is not based on instructions and theories that are taught in a lot of popular credit repair books. Many of those books teach consumers to pay any outstanding debts you owe and magically your credit score will increase and your credit repaired. Those instructions and theories are far from the truth.

Whenever a consumer is trying to rebuild or repair their credit which may have resulted in a personal financial hardship, there are two activities that have to work simultaneously in order to maximize the success in achieving good personal credit. The two activities are how to negotiate your debts with creditors and the how to have those negotiated results appear on your credit report to increase your credit score. Just paying your debts will not increase your credit score, that's a lie that creditors tell consumers to convince them to pay their debts. I am not advocating to not paying your personal debts, but I am advocating for consumers to learn the proper strategies that will benefit them financially.

This book is written in two parts, in Part I "Become Aware and Learn your Rights" the book explains to you the importance of having better credit and the benefits for consumers. It also examines the use of a consumer's credit report and the role that the government has taken to educate and protect the general public on the laws of credit reporting.

Part II of the book "Negotiate and Settle your Debts", will begin to instruct you on how to remove any derogatory information that exists on your credit report; by leveraging the laws written in Part I regarding the role of the FDCPA and FCRA. This book will also provide you with 10 Credit Dispute letters; it is not necessary to recreate your own letters, just use the ones that are provided in the Appendix section of this book

By the end of this book you will understand and learn:

- How to deal with harassing debt collectors.

- How to settle a debt with a debt collector and increase your credit score.

- How the FDCPA and the FCRA can help consumers with debt settlement.

- Why paying old debts will do nothing to increase your credit score and rebuild your credit.

- Why bankruptcy should be your last option.

Jump Start Your Credit: How to Negotiate and Settle your Debts in 10 Steps

Contents

Jump Start Your Credit:
How to Negotiate and Settle your Debts in 10 Steps

PART I

Become Aware and Learn
Your Rights

Jump Start Your Credit:
How to Negotiate and Settle your Debts in 10 Steps

Step 1   The First Step in Rebuilding Credit

Using your personal credit can be one of the most intimidating endeavors an individual may experience during the course of their lifetime. Establishing and maintaining credit can put a consumer through a maze of confusion; there is so much to understand, for example fixed and variable interest rate, APR, credit limit, etc. When an individual has not mastered the usage of personal credit their chances of default is heighten.

Trying to rebound from defaulted credit which has left a paper trail of derogatory information on your credit report can be difficult to rebuild. Many individuals do not know how to properly go forward with reestablishing good credit. Before a consumer can begin the process of rebuilding their credit, the first place to start is find out where you stand with your personal credit. The first step in the credit rebuilding process is to obtain your credit report and credit score from the three credit reporting agencies. The three credit reporting agencies in the US are Experian, Equifax and TransUnion. Each credit report agency will always contain information that may be different from one report, that's why it is always important to order all three credit reports.

Receiving your credit report and credit score

There is no charge to receive your credit report; you can order your credit report from either 1 of 3 ways. You can receive your credit report by calling a toll free number, mail order form, or use the credit bureau's online website request tool. Keep in mind if you decide to use a mail order form, you will have to submit a copy of your drivers license to prove your identity. If you are looking to access all three credit report right away the best way is by using the website http://www.annualcreditreport.com it will provide you links to all three credit bureaus, but there is a fee to receive your credit score. Also for disputing purposes you cannot use the credit reports released from the annualcreditreport.com website, only credit reports that were physically mailed to a consumer by the credit bureaus can be used.

If you decide to order your credit report and want to receive your credit score. You will have to pay an additional fee. The fees for all three credit bureaus do vary so the price is not the same. Many credit bureaus are now using the Vantage scoring model to determine a consumer's credit score. In the past the FICO scoring model was used widely by the credit bureaus, but in 2006 when the Vantage Score was released it is now being used as a credit scoring tool used by the credit bureaus. What's the difference between FICO and Vantage score? The difference between the two credit scoring models is the credit scoring algorithm. FICO uses a credit scoring algorithm that ranges from 300 to 850 and Vantage Score has an algorithm that ranges from 501 to 990 as well as a letter grade of A to F for each scoring range.

Who are "Big Three"

When ordering and disputing your credit report information it is important to know the names of the three major credit bureaus along with their contact information. I have listed all the necessary information a consumer will need to request a copy of their credit report. In order to dispute errors on your credit report, you can easily contact the three organizations by mail, telephone, or through the Internet:

Equifax Credit Information Services, Inc
P.O. Box 740241

Atlanta, GA 30374 Telephone:
1-888-766-0008
Online: www.equifax.com

TransUnion LLC Consumer Disclosure Center
P.O. Box 1000
Chester, PA 19022 Telephone:
1-800-888-4213
Online: www.transunion.com

Experian National Consumer Assistance Center
 PO Box 2002
Allen, TX 75013
Telephone: 1-888-397-3742
Online: www.experian.com

Consequences for bad credit

Having bad credit limits your choices not only do you get turned
down for major purchases which may require credit. You also
limit your chances for employment; many employers make their
hiring decisions based on if a person has a good credit history.

Employers who use credit history as a hiring tool believe that a
person's character is based on how well they pay their debt
obligations. Even employees who are actually hired, employers
are taking a proactive approach with working with employees
who have debt problems and bad credit. Statistics show that
individuals who are facing a financial hardship are more prone to
stealing and company embezzlement.

Whenever you apply for a job there is a good chance you future
employer may ask to do a background check. When you consent
to a background check, which gives the potential employer the
ability to access your credit report, that's why it's important to
order your credit report every year. Employers are looking to

see how you pays your bills, are they paid on time, are the bills delinquent, are there any public record information for example bankruptcies, judgments or tax liens. Even if you are hired by an employer, your credit report can used to make future decisions regarding an employee's promotion, retention and reassignment.

Quick fact: According to the US Department of Labor, an employer can terminate an employee if he or she has had a wage garnishment more than one time. All second and subsequent wage garnishments are grounds for an employee to be discharged.

Knowing is essential

When you decide to take the journey to rebuild your credit it's important that you examine your credit report closely once you receive the report. You want to examine your credit report because you want to look for any inaccuracies that may be in your credit report that could harm your chance for receiving new credit or getting a job. If you find any inaccuracies, you have the right to request an investigation. I always recommend that you do an investigation in writing to the credit bureaus. Once you have requested that a particular item in your credit history be investigated, the agency must respond within 30 days providing documentation of the entry in question. If they fail to do so, the entry must be removed from your credit report. Always keep a paper trail of your investigation request. All investigation requests should be done certified return receipt through US mail.

It is important to know that if you are having an item investigated that you have some supporting information to support the claim. The credit bureaus are not interested in you improving your credit; credit bureaus are not governmental agencies. They are companies who are in business to generate a profit, and it is big business when a consumer has bad credit. Many credit bureaus sell the consumers personal information, that's why consumers are always bombarded with credit offers in the mail.

Conclusion

I know the information that I am providing may seem overwhelming and can be burdensome, but it is absolutely important that you obtain your credit report to examine what is being reported before you even attempt to settle your debts. If you do not examine your credit report before you decide to negotiate or settle your debts, the decision that is made may be only advantageous for the debt collector and the credit bureau, you want the decision to benefit you as the consumer. Knowledge of these things is important and essential in order to begin to be effective with the process of credit rebuilding.

Jump Start Your Credit:
How to Negotiate and Settle your Debts in 10 Steps

Step 2   Your Credit Report Demystified

The information that is within your credit report is personal and
financially sensitive. How that information is reported can
determine your creditworthiness. The FCRA which stands for
Fair Credit Reporting Act is a consumer protection agency
created by the Federal Trade Commission (FTC). The purpose
of the federal Fair Credit Reporting Act (FCRA) is to promote
the accuracy, fairness, and privacy of information in the files of
consumer reporting agencies. In 2003, the FCRA was extended
with additional legislation; the legislation that was passed was
called the FACT Act or FACTA Act.

The FACT or FACTA Act

The FACTA Act which stands for **Fair and Accurate Credit
Transactions Act** was signed into law by President Bush on
December 2003. The new legislation that was passed
superseded a large portion of the FCRA, along with added some
new information that was never address in the FCRA. Here are
some of the key areas of the FACTA Act:

- Identity Theft Prevention
- Use of Consumer Disputes
- Truncation of Credit cards, Debit cards, Social Security
  Numbers

Identity Theft Prevention

Before the FACTA Act was passed in 2003, there was no
legislation to protect consumers whose identity had been stolen.
According to the FTC, there were 10 million people who were
affected by identity theft in 2002. Although identity theft is a

serious crime, there are precautions consumers can take to prevent themselves from being a victim of identity theft.

- Do not throw away any bills in the trash that may contain credit or debit cards account numbers.
- Examine bank, credit and debit cards statements on a regular basis to locate any unusual spending patterns or unauthorized charges.
- Do not give personal or financial information over the phone or email.
- When shopping or banking online, use websites that protect your financial information with encryption. Look for an encrypted site has "https" at the beginning of the web address; "s" is for secure.

Use of Consumer Disputes

A furnisher of credit is what the FCRA defines as a user who can access a consumer's credit report. Any personal or financial information that is reported on the credit report is deemed to be true, which is why if a consumer realizes some of the information that is being reported is not correct he or she has the right to dispute the information being reported. When the FACTA Act was passed there were two sections that addressed the accuracy and the integrity of what was being reported.

- The accuracy guidelines for financial institutions and creditors that furnish information to credit bureaus.
- The ability of consumers to dispute information with companies that report to credit bureaus.

What this means is, there is legislation put in place that if a company wants to report information to a credit reporting agency, they must be accurate that the information is correct. The furnisher of credit cannot report the information if there is

10

knowledge of any errors being reported. So if a consumer has a dispute because information is not correct, the credit bureaus must correct those errors immediately. Consumers also have the right to dispute those errors with the company directly.

Truncation of Credit cards, Debit cards, Social Security Numbers

Whenever you make a purchase with your credit or debit card, your credit card receipt will only have the last four numbers printed on the receipt. When the FACTA Act was passed companies that accept credit or debit cards for payment, are only allowed to print the last four numbers of the consumer's credit or debit card, the act also prohibited companies from including the card's expiration date. Regarding social security numbers, users who request the SSN of a consumer are only allowed to include the last four digits not all nine numbers.

Conclusion

How can all this information help you? Whenever there are errors in your credit report that you may not recognize, it could be a single different digit or even a space between characters would completely alter what is being reported. That's why it's important for consumers to order the free credit report from all three credit bureaus, that they are entitled to once a year. If a consumer notices that there is inaccurate information being reported on their credit report they have the right to dispute those inaccuracies with the credit bureau and the furnisher who's reporting the false information. It is important that you understand, that anything can be disputed on your credit report, which means multiple addresses of where you previous lived, different variations of your first and last name, as well credit accounts you no longer own. It is critical that you examine the information on your credit report at least once during the year, using this precaution could save you from identity theft, and incorrect reporting credit trade lines within your credit report.

Step 3 Understanding Important Parts of your Credit Report

At this point I have explained to you the importance of ordering your credit report and why it's necessary to examine your credit report for any errors. This chapter will explain and help you to understand the information that is within your credit report. Don't be ashamed if you do not understand what your reading, many people are just like you, they have a hard time understanding what items on an actual credit report represent, let alone interpreting all of the information it contains. Once you are done with this chapter you will feel more confident the next time you read your credit report. Although each credit reporting agency may have a slightly different format, all credit reports contain basically the same categories of information. Here are basic categories of information found in your credit report.

Personal Identifying Information

Your personal identifying information is within the end of the credit report, there you will find your name, address, SSN, date of birth, and employment information, which is used to identify you. In that area you may have multiple versions of your name, especially if you are a married/divorced female who has changed her name a few times. This section will also show any nicknames and abbreviations of you name that might be luring out there. Your past and present address (es) will be included as well. These factors are not used in credit scoring. But it is important to correct any inaccuracies of the information, if you no longer live at an old address request to have it removed from your credit report that also includes the different variations of your name.

Trade Lines

There are different credit accounts listed on your credit report each line item within the credit report is established within either a lenders or card holder. Lenders and cardholders are suppose to report the type of account, the date you opened the account, your credit limit, your loan amount, the account balance, and your payment history.

Here are the different types of trade line account classifications that are listed within a credit report:

- **Mortgage Accounts.** These include first mortgages, home equity loans, and any other loans secured by real estate that you own.
- **Revolving Accounts.** Revolving accounts are credit card charge accounts that have a credit limit and require a minimum payment each month. These are your Visa, MasterCard, American Express and department store cards.
- **Installment Accounts.** Installment accounts are credit accounts in which the amount of the payment and the number of payments are predetermined or fixed, such as a car loan.
- Student Loan Accounts – accounts that were established to repay loans used for college.

Credit Inquiries

Whenever you apply for a loan, the potential lender will always have to request a copy of your credit report. Once that request is made an inquiry will appear on your credit report. Inquiries that appear on your credit reports are categorized as either voluntary or involuntary credit inquiries; voluntary and involuntary inquires are also referred to as "hard" and "soft" inquiries.

An example of a voluntary "hard "credit inquiry is when you apply for a credit card or a loan, once you made the authorization to apply for credit an inquiry will appear on your personal credit report; voluntary inquiries stay on your credit report for 2 years. Involuntary "soft" credit inquiries occur when a current creditor accesses your credit report to see how you are paying your current creditors; the creditor is looking to see if there are any late pays or credit accounts in default. You will also find inquires that appear on your credit report that you did not authorized.

Companies that order you report that may not be familiar to you are usually companies that will send you "Pre-Approved" offers in the mail. It is important to follow up with the companies to have them to remove the inquiry from your credit report. Listed below is a letter that you can send to a company that involuntarily accessed your credit report without your authorization.

Creditor Company Name
Company Address
Company City, State Zip

Re: Unauthorized Credit Inquiry

    Dear Creditor,

       I recently received a copy of my Experian credit report. The   credit report showed a credit inquiry by your company that I do not recall authorizing. I understand that you should not be allowed to put an inquiry on my file unless I have authorized it. Please have this

inquiry removed from my credit file because it
is making it very
difficult for me to acquire credit.

I have sent this letter certified mail
because I need your prompt
response to this issue immediately. Please be
so kind as to forward me   documentation that
you have had the unauthorized inquiry removed.

If you find that I am incorrect, and you did
have my authorization to inquire into my credit
report, then please send me proof of this
authorization.

Thank you in advance,

Your Name

Public Record Accounts

On all three credit reports whether it is Experian, Equifax or
TransUnion the public records accounts will always be listed in
the beginning of the credit report. Public records accounts are
judgments, federal and state tax liens, Credit reporting agencies
also collect public record information from state and county
courts, and information on overdue debt from collection
agencies. Public record information includes bankruptcies,
foreclosures, suits, wage attachments, liens and judgments.

Satisfactory Accounts and Negatives Items

All three of the major credit reporting agencies (TransUnion,
Equifax, and Experian) will segregate "positive" accounts from
"negative" ones, thereby making the interpretation of your report
a little easier. The Equifax report gives a nice "Credit Summary"

16

which provides a one-page, easy to review snapshot of all your open accounts, as well as some useful summary statistics, such as total debt by account type, debt to credit ratio by account type, and length of credit history.

In the section showing the negative items, these accounts will be listed showing when a late payment occurred and how late is was, the balance on these accounts, and if this account was a charge-off or went to a collection agency. It will usually have the address of the creditor and the account number listed as well.

Credit Report Formats and Codes

Within each credit report of the three credit bureaus they all have report layouts that may be similar, but there are some differences within the three reports. If you want to know how to decipher the credit report in it's entirely, you can go to a website called creditengine.net which provides each of the three credit bureau report layouts and an explanation of all the codes found on each report. What is interesting about this website is that it will deciphers the payment history codes, the public record codes, the trade check rating codes, and breaks down each section of the report. If there is anything on your credit report you do not understand, go to one of the links below and you will find out what all the codes mean.

- Experian Credit Report Format and Codes
- TransUnion Credit Report Format and Codes
- Equifax Credit Report Format and Codes

Common Questions about your Credit Report

Listed below are some common questions that you may have regarding your credit report. I know you may have other questions but this is a thorough list and it should cover all your credit report questions.

Is it necessary for me to check my credit report several times a year? Many states will allow consumers to order a free credit once a year, but if you are currently disputing information on your credit report, all three credit bureaus will continue to send you updated credit reports until you have fully disputed the information.

Why are my three credit reports and credit scores different? Comparing all three credit reports and credit scores will always be different; the credit bureaus do not share information with each other. Your goal as a consumer is not to dispute the information to make it identical within the three reports, but to dispute the information that is incorrect which could potentially lower your credit score.

Why is it important to know my credit score? Whenever you make a major purchase, for example buying a house or a car; your credit score will be used to determine if the lender will approve the transaction. So often consumers have no idea where their score ranges, when a consumer know credit score and how it works. That consumer will have more negotiating power, because he or she know that higher credit scores favor better interest rates for major purchases.

I am married will my spouse's information appear on my credit report? Your personal credit report will contain only your credit and loan accounts, but if the two of you have joint accounts. The accounts that the two of you have jointly will appear on each of your accounts separately. The information will also be reported, if either one of you co-signed on a credit account.

What is "Account Balance" on a credit report? This is the amount that is owed on the loan currently or within the last 30 days. The amount could represent a credit card balance, automobile loan, student loan or installment loan.

What is "High Balance" on a credit report? This is the highest amount ever owed on the credit line; this amount could also include any interest, penalties or fees that could have accrued on the account.

What is "Credit Limit" on a credit report? This is the amount that you were approved for as a credit line. The credit line could be used for a credit card, automobile loan, or installment loan.

What is "Date of Last Activity" (DOLA)? This will be specified on the report as "last updated' or "last activity" and basically is the last date any account activity occurred, typically the last time you made a payment on the credit account.

What does "Account Closed by Credit Grantor" mean? The credit card company that issued you the credit line was afraid that you would default on the debt and shut down your ability to access any more of your credit line. Many times this happens because a creditor notices that you have already defaulted on other credit cards.

Should I add a"100 word statement" to my credit report, if I disagree with the disputing results? I am not an advocate for adding the statement to your credit report; keep in mind whenever a consumer decides to add the statement, the furnisher who can extend credit will pull your credit report to make a decision; which will include the statement that you added. Further adding a "100 word statement" will not improve your credit score or help to eliminate derogatory listed on your credit report.

Jump Start Your Credit:
How to Negotiate and Settle your Debts in 10 Steps

Step 4   The FDCPA, FCRA and The 2009 Credit Card Act

Whenever a consumer commits to the credit rebuilding process it is important to know that there are laws established by the Federal government to protect consumers. The Fair Debt Collection Practices Act (FDCPA) is a consumer's best friend; the FDCPA protects consumers from debt collectors. Many debt collectors use harsh collection practices to collect debts from consumers, which are illegal and I will go further into this topic later. The FCRA is a short acronym for the Fair Credit Reporting Act; the FCRA regulates how information is reported on your personal credit report.   If you would a thorough explanation of the FCRA, go back and revisit chapter 2 this book.

What are the FDCPA and FCRA?

The Fair Debt Collections Practices Act (FDCPA) has 19 code sections that consumers need to know in order to be successful when fighting with debt collectors and eliminating items on their credit report.   Here are three of the most important statues that will assist you with defeating debt collections:

- **805 Communication in connection with debt collection.** This relates to how a debt collector can communicate with a consumer and the time day a debt collector can call a consumer home.
- **806 Harassment or abuse.** Debt collectors are not suppose to harass, threaten or abuse consumers
- **809 Validation of debts.** Consumers have the right to know the validity of a debt, and a letter stating this law is suppose to be sent to a consumer 5 days after the initial communication.

Jump Start Your Credit:
How to Negotiate and Settle your Debts in 10 Steps

When you decide to communicate with a debt collectors whether it is over the phone or by mail, it is important you know your rights. Do not be the consumer who does not know the law and falls prey to whatever the debt collector may say. It is also important to be on the opposite side of the spectrum and just ignore any correspondence that send in the mail; and what about the phone calls, do not ignore those either later in the book I will tell how you can stop any phone calls immediately. Dealing with debt collectors do not have to be imitating in the Section II part of this book I will go more in depth with how the FDCPA can help you with the credit rebuilding and fighting debt collectors.

The Fair Credit Reporting Act (FCRA) provides the law and statues on how information should be reported on your credit report. It also provides the law on information being reported correctly and that credit reporting agencies have a duty to follow the law. The FCRA has 29 statues, and its purpose is to promote the accuracy, fairness, and privacy of information in the files of consumer reporting agencies. In chapter 2, I went discussed in detail why the FCRA is a critical piece when you discover inaccurate items being reported on your credit report. I also went into detail about how the FCRA was extended with the FACT ACT which was put in place in 2003. If you want to refresh yourself on the information I provided on the FCRA go back to chapter 2. . The main areas of the act were thoroughly discussed in chapter 2 which are:

- **Identity Theft Prevention**
- **Use of Consumer Disputes**
- **Truncation of Credit cards, Debit cards, Social Security Numbers**

What the above all means is as a consumer you have the right to dispute any derogatory information with a credit reporting agency. That incorrect information may be furnished by any company that reports any negative information on your credit report that includes debt collection agencies.

In 2011, congress added another piece of legislation to extend the law for the FDCPA and the FCRA; this added legislation is called the Consumer Financial Protection Bureau (CFPB). The CFPB acts as a government enforcer to ensure consumers have a place to educate themselves on the practices of debt collection and credit reporting. According to the CFPB.gov website, the CFPB role is to ensure that consumers get the information they need to make financial decisions that they believe are best for themselves and their families.

At this point you're thinking okay how will this information help me, well later in this book I will discuss with you how the FDCPA and the FCRA will help you when you're disputing and negotiating your debts.

The 2009 Credit Card Act

The **Credit Card Accountability Responsibility and Disclosure Act of 2009** also known as the **Credit Card Act of 2009** is a federal statute passed by the United States Congress and signed by President Barack Obama on May 22, 2009. This act provides comprehensive credit card reform legislation that aims to establish fair and transparent practices relating to the extension of personal credit to consumers. What this all means is that the government wants to ensure that individuals are being responsible when they apply for a personal credit card. Many individuals do not understand the contractual agreement that has been signed between them and the credit card company, and that is what this book will explain in Part II. According to the Credit Card Act of 2009, here are some of the key points consumers should know about the act:

- Cardholders have protections against interest rate increases
- Cardholders who pay on time should not be penalized
- Cardholders should be protected from due date gimmicks
- Cardholders should be protected from misleading terms
- Cardholders deserve the right to set limits on their credit
- Card companies should fairly credit and allocate payments
- Vulnerable consumers should be protected from fee-heavy subprime credit cards
- Minimum payment explanation
- Limits credit cards to teens
- Internet posting of credit card agreements

Conclusion

A large part of what you learned in this chapter and the previous chapters will be revisited in the following section of this book in Part II. In the next section I will share with you how the FDCPA and the FCRA will assists consumers with fighting debts and rebuilding their credits. It's important to go back and forth so you can see how this correlation will help get your credit on track.

PART II

NEGOTIATE AND SETTLE YOUR DEBTS

Jump Start Your Credit:
How to Negotiate and Settle your Debts in 10 Steps

Step 5 Recognizing the Different Types of Debts

This chapter will lay the foundation for you to be able to distinguish and identify your debts that are being reported on your credit report. It's important to know the three types of personal debts, before you commit to any debt settlement or debt consolidation to improve your credit. It's important you understand how these three debts work.

> 1. **Current Debts.** Current debts are debts that are being paid on a timely basis, during a 30 day period. These debts are not past due.
> 2. **Past Due Debts.** These are debts are past the 30 day paying cycle and are 45, 60 or 90 days old.
> 3. **Defaulted/Charged off Debts.** Debts that have not been paid in over 120 – 180 days.

Current Debts
These are debts that you are currently paying on that are not being collected by a debt collector. An example these debts would be revolving accounts (credit cards), installment accounts, and mortgage accounts. In chapter 3, I explained how these type of accounts work, and gave you a explanation. Current debts are debts that have a 30 days cycle, as long as you pay the accounts during the cycle you will not risk the creditor reporting you late to the credit bureau.

Past Due Debts
Past Due Debts are debts that are past the 30 day payment cycle, once you go beyond 45 days a creditor can report you late to the credit bureaus. Even though the payments can be caught up to be current any payments that are 45, 60 or 90 days are considered late.

Defaulted/Charged off Debts

Individuals', who are trying to rebound from bad credit, should understand that 80% to 90% of their bad credit will be made up of Defaulted/Charged off collection accounts.
Defaulted/Charged off debts are the debts that can ruin your credit report and credit score. These debts are also being collected by companies who do not have the legal responsibility to collect on the debts. These are debts that 120 - 180 days past due, once a creditor see that a consumer account has gone past 120 days they will sell account off to a debt collector.

If you want to rebuild your credit it is important to understand how to deal with debt collectors, you do not want to just pay a debt collector the debt without knowing what is the law. That is why this book is different from other credit rebuilding books, this book instructs consumers with the how and what to fight debt collectors back to accomplish having better personal credit.

Once you have finished reading this chapter you will understand why it's important to know the law. I hope you have not skipped Part I of this book. In order for you to understand the information being discussed later you have to understand, how debtor collection process works and the language that is used to by debt collectors to collect on any outstanding debts.

Should I pay my outstanding Defaulted/Charged off Debts

The credit rebuilding process can be a daunting task and before you anxiously decide to pay an outstanding debt that you have notice on your credit report, or a collection letter that you have received in the mail. It is important that you understand who are the key players and their role when you are paying an outstanding bill. It is important to know the difference between Original Creditors, Collection Agencies and Junk Debt Buyers.

Who are and what are Original Creditors, Collections Agencies and Junk Debt Buyers? Why Do I care?

In the beginning part of this chapter I described to you the different types of debts that consumers must recognize on their credit report before they make a plan to eliminate any debts on their credit report. If you have identified on your credit report that some of your personal debts are defaulted and charged off. This means those debts are owned by a collection agency, which many consumers refer to as "bill collectors". Before I go into a thorough explanation on how collection agencies work I have to give you a clear distinction of an original creditor and a collection agency.

Original Creditors are the credit card companies that issued you (the debtor) the credit card to make purchases. For example those cards maybe American Express, Discover, VISA, MasterCard or department store cards (e.g. Macys, Lord & Taylor, Sears etc.)

Collection Agency (ies) are companies that buy unpaid debts from Original Creditors. These unpaid debts are charged off by the Original Creditor because the consumer has not paid on the debts for as long as 90-120 days. This also includes attorney offices that collect on debts as well.

Junk Debt Buyers is another name for a collection agencies, these companies specialize in purchasing old collection accounts from credit card companies that are older than 120 to 180 days old. These debts may be credit cards, auto loans, telecommunication accounts, or retail accounts. Junk Debt Buyers buy unpaid and outstanding credit accounts from the original creditor in bulk for pennies on the dollar, which is why they can offer the consumer discounts off their outstanding bill.

Jump Start Your Credit:
How to Negotiate and Settle your Debts in 10 Steps

Here is an example:

If you have a charged off balance of $3,500 that was once owned by American Express the JDB will purchased that debt for .20 cents on the dollar which means the JDB paid only $700 dollars. Now you see why collection companies can offer you a discount off of what you owed. They can offer a discount on the debt because the JDB did not pay a lot for the debt. The price of what a debt collector pays on a debt varies, but the cost is not a lot of money.

Debts that are listed on your credit report that lower your credit score are mostly debt collection accounts, which I listed in the beginning of this chapter as defaulted debts. Defaulted debts can cause the most harm to your credit report and credit score.

Here below taken from FTC.gov website are fines and that were imposed on a Debt Collector also know as a Junk Debt Buyer in Las Vegas:

> **In 2008, Academy Collection Service, Inc. and its owner, Keith Dickstein, paid $2.25 million to settle FTC charges that Academy collectors violated the FTC Act and the FDCPA while collecting debts, and that Dickstein failed to stop the violations. The settlement order announced today, negotiated by DOJ and the FTC, imposed civil penalties of $375,000 and $300,000, respectively, on Albert S. Bastian and Edward Hurt, who oversaw Academy's Las Vegas collection center. The judgments were suspended upon payment of $7,500 each, based on their ability to pay. The full judgments will become due immediately if the defendants are found to have misrepresented their financial condition. Source taken from www.ftc.gov 11/7/2010**

Step 6   Unfair and Harassing Behaviors by Collection Agencies

It is important that you know your rights as consumer because some Collection Agencies operate in an unfair matter, it is essential that you understand your rights regarding how collection agency can contact you.

Let's assume you owe money on a debt, the debt that you owe is now charged off by the Original Creditor as well as you defaulted on the debt. The debt which was once owed by the Original Creditor has been sold and purchased by the Collection Agency. Since the collection agency now owns the debt, they begin using unlawful tactics to get you to pay debt.

Although a collection agency may have the right to collect on a debt that you owe, there is a manner of protocol they have to following according to the Federal Trade Commission (FTC). The FTC is part of the federal government and they provide rules that collection agencies must follow in order to collect on a debt.

Many consumers do not know that it is illegal and unlawful for collection agencies to use harsh tactics to persuade a consumer to pay a debt. It is your right as a consumer to remind debt collectors that they are not allowed to threaten or harass you to pay a debt.

As a consumer it is important that you know your rights Collection Agencies, Debt Collectors and Junk Buyers are not allowed to do the following:

- Call your office or place of employment
- Call your home before 8 a.m. or after 9 p.m.
- Address you in an abusive manner

31

- Call family or friends in an attempt to collect your debt
- Harass or threaten you to pay a debt
- Call you neighbors home in an attempt to collect your debt
- Threaten to send you to court
- Make false or misleading statements
- Add unauthorized charges

If any of the above incidents are happening to you, tell the collection agency to stop harassing you. Explain to them that you know your rights as a consumer and that they are violating the laws of the FTC to collect on the debt. If the harassment continues, ask for the name or address of the debt collector and report the company to the Better Business Bureau, the Federal Trade Commission (FTC) or your state's attorney general's office.

The Fair Debt Collection Practices Act (FDCPA) which is the Federal agency that protects consumers from debt collectors states that you can demand that the collection agency stop contacting you; unless they are contacting you to let you know that the collection efforts have ended or that the creditor or collection agency will sue you. In Chapter 4, I told you that there are 19 code sections in the FDCPA, the two that relate to communication and harassment are:

- **805 Communication in connection with debt collection.** This relates to how a debt collector can communicate with a consumer and the time day a debt collector can call a consumer home.
- **806 Harassment or abuse.** Debt collectors are not suppose to harass, threaten or abuse consumers

However, if you want them to stop contacting you must put your request in writing.

Listed below is taken from the FTC.gov regarding how Debt Collectors should communicate with consumers:

"The FTC wants to remind debt collectors of their responsibilities and obligations under the law. Abusive collection actions are illegal, and if debt collectors use abusive tactics they could face legal action," Director of the FTC's Bureau of Consumer Protection. "At the same time, we want consumers to understand their rights if their debts go into collection. Money matters and the more people know about managing their debt and dealing with debt collectors, the better off they will be." Source taken from www.FTC.gov website

It's important to note: That the rules, that the FTC's FDCPA has put forth to protect consumers only apply to bill collectors who work for collection agencies, not the original creditors. You will not be able to get the collection department of a credit card company to stop calling you with a letter. Only in some states, will the local law allow a consumer to write to contact an original creditor to stop any communication regarding an outstanding debt.

Here below is the letter that you would use to stop the harassing calls from a collection agency: *(There is a letter like this for you to use in the Appendix section of this book)*

Cease and Desist letter

ABC Collection Agency
123 Main St
Anytown, NJ 07888

17 April 2012

RE: Account 87654690

Dear Sir or Madam:

I request that you CEASE and DESIST in your efforts to collect on the
above referenced account. It is my personal policy not to deal with collection agencies and I will only deal with the original creditor of this account.

You are hereby instructed to cease collection efforts immediately or
face legal sanctions under applicable Federal and State law.

GIVE THIS LETTER THE IMMEDIATE ATTENTION IT DESERVES

Cordially,

Jane Doe

Step 7   What is Debt Validation?

Debt Validation is a consumer's best friend, and a consumer secret weapon for dealing with debt collectors. In the previous chapter I discussed with you, how the FDCPA which is an agency of the FTC has legally provided rules on how collection agencies and debt collectors can contact you. This chapter will provide you with one of the most powerful strategies that can be used by a consumer when they are dealing with a debt collector.

When a consumer is contacted by a debt collector the correspondence is communicated in one or three ways: a letter in the mail, a listing on your credit report or a telephone call. Debt Validation is a legal procedure which has been put into law by the FTC they agency that handles the law regarding rules pertaining to debt validation is the Fair Debt Collection Practices Act (FDCPA).

In chapter 4 of this book, I briefly discussed the role of the FDCPA. I also mention that there are 19 code sections of the FDCPA. The code section of law that relates to debt validation is code section 809.

- **809 Validation of debts.** Consumers have the right to know the validity of a debt, and a letter stating this law is suppose to be sent to a consumer 5 days after the initial communication.

It is important that you understand the rules that are set forth in the FDCPA do not apply to original creditors only debt collectors. So the information that I will share with you, is related to debt collectors. The debt validation strategy can only help you against debt collectors.

What is debt validation?

Debt validation is proof that must be supplied by the debt collector that shows that they can legally collect on a debt. Remember the code section in 809 says a consumer has the right to know the validity of the debt in other words that means that a debt collector must provide proof to a consumer that they can collect on a debt.

So what that means to you as a consumer, that before you pay any debt that is now owned by a debt collector, you have a right to know if they can legally collect on the debt.

If you are wondering what type of proof is necessary to show validation from the debt collector.

Here is a list of items a debt collector must provide to show in the debt validation process.

- Proof that the collection company owns the debt/or has been assigned the debt. You want to know if the debt collector legally entitled to collect this particular debt from you. A legal binding contract between the debt collector and the original creditor.
- You want to request some account statements from the original creditor. If you really want to get specific, you can pin them down on the amount of the debt by requiring complete payment history, starting with the original creditor. You want to see all of the fees/interest that was tacked on by the debt collector.
- A copy of the original signed loan agreement or credit card application, or you settle on the account statements from the original creditor, which can fulfill these requirements.

Jump Start Your Credit:
How to Negotiate and Settle your Debts in 10 Steps

Understand when a debt collector is providing proof that they owned the debt, the debt collecting company has to use statements and documents from the original creditor. Many debt collectors try to send statements that have been created by the collection company; those statements do not suffice as proof in validating a debt.

Whenever you are requesting to validate a debt by a debt collector you always want to put your request in writing in a letter. The letter should be sent by certified return receipt, which means you will have a paper trail that you sent the debt collector the letter.

(Here is a sample Debt Validation letter that you can send to debt collector to validate the debt.)

Debt Validation Letter

Date

Your Name
Your Address
City, State Zip

Collection Agency
Collection Agency Address
City, State Zip

Re: Acct # XXXX-XXXX-XXXX-XXXX

To Whom It May Concern:

I am sending this letter to you in response to a notice I received from you on (*date of letter*). Be advised, this is not a refusal to pay, but a notice sent pursuant to the Fair

37

Debt Collection Practices Act, 15 USC 1692g Sec. 809 (b) that your claim is disputed and validation is requested.

This is NOT a request for "verification" or proof of my mailing address, but a request for VALIDATION made pursuant to the above named Title and Section. I respectfully request that your office provide me with competent evidence that I have any legal obligation to pay you.

Please provide me with the following:

- What the money you say I owe is for;
- Explain and show me how you calculated what you say I owe;
- Provide me with copies of any papers that show I agreed to pay what you say I owe;
- Provide a verification or copy of any judgment if applicable;
- Identify the original creditor;
- Prove the Statute of Limitations has not expired on this account;
- Show me that you are licensed to collect in my state; and
- Provide me with your license numbers and Registered Agent.

If your offices fail to respond to this validation request within 30 days from the date of your receipt, all references to this account must be deleted and completely removed from my credit file and a copy of such deletion request shall be sent to me immediately.

I would also like to request, in writing, that no telephone contact be made by your offices to my home or to my place of employment. If your offices attempt telephone communication with me, including but not limited to computer generated calls or corresponcence sent to any third parties, it will be corsidered harassment and I will have no choice but to file suit. All future communications with me MUST be done in writing and sent to the address noted in this letter.

This is an attempt to correct your records; any information obtained shall be used for that purpose.

Best Regards,

Your Name

Do you have a right to request a "Debt Validation" from a debt collector?

Yes and I mean absolutely, under the FDCPA, you are allowed to asked the debt collector to validate the debt, and the creditor (in this case, the collection agency) must show you proof that you owe the debt to the collection agency (not to the original creditor.) Here is a section of the FDCPA that describes what debt collectors must do:

FDCPA Section 809. Validation of debts [15 USC 1692g](b) If the consumer notifies the debt collector in writing within the thirty-day period described in subsection (a) that the debt, or any portion thereof, is disputed, or that the consumer requests the name and address of the original creditor, the debt collector shall cease collection of the debt, or any disputed portion thereof, until the debt collector obtains verification of the debt or any copy of a judgment, or the name and address of the original creditor, and a

copy of such verification or judgment, or name and address of the original creditor, is mailed to the consumer by the debt collector.

Keep in mind a debt collector cannot ask you to pay for them to dig up this information, also do not accept some computer generated print out of what they said you owe; that will not suffice.

In conclusion, I have explained to you the debt validation process and what is debt validation. If a creditor cannot validate a debt, they are not allowed to do the following:

- They are not allowed to collect the debt,
- They are not allowed to contact you about the debt,
- They are also not allowed to report it under the Fair Credit Reporting Act (FCRA). Doing so is a violation of the FCRA, and the FCRA states that you can sue for $1,000 in damages for any violation of the Act.

Step 8   Should I settle my Debts? Debt Settlement

Before you begin to settle your debts with a company who has contacted you about the debt, it is important you understand who still owns the debt. In chapter 5, I explained to you why it is important to know the lifecycle of the debt. Once you know what cycle the debt is currently in, for example is the debt owed a current debt or a defaulted debt; then you will know what strategy you can use to settle with the creditor.

In the previous chapters, I explained to you the difference between an Original Creditor and a Debt Collector, but there are different strategies that apply to each party. Finding out who owns the debt is simple, if the collection agency is calling you regarding your outstanding debt with Amex, VISA, MC, Discover or a department store credit card. Then that means the original creditor no longer owns the debt. If want to be certain that the original creditor no longer owes the outstanding debt, you can call the original creditor customer service department, the agent of the credit card company will gladly explain to you if debt has been sold to an outside party, which is a collection agency.

When an original creditor sells a debt to a collection agency they have legally cut their ties to the debt. Understand the original creditor has received all the tax benefits that are associated with selling off bad debt, so that means the original creditor has no interested in dealing with a consumer who has defaulted on a past due debt.

Jump Start Your Credit:
How to Negotiate and Settle your Debts in 10 Steps

Why do most consumers hit the panic button and settle with collection agencies?

Because many consumers are unaware of their rights when they deal with collection agencies, and many fear that they will get sued. That is why it is important to understand the rules and laws that protect consumers in the FDCPA Section **809 Validation of Debts.**

One of the most widely used fear tactics used by collection agencies is the threat of suing the consumer. Yes being sued is a reality, but if you understand how Debt Validation can assist you with fighting a debt collector, it can prevent you from being sued by the collection agency. When a debt collector decides to sue a consumer the lawsuit filings can be a lengthy process in some US states. You can avoid being sued by answering the court notice, and proving to the court that the debt collector violated the laws of the FDCPA by not validating the debt.

If you decide not to answer a court notice, because you fear what could happen, you are only giving ammunition to the collection agency to win a judgment against you. Once this happens you will lose all your rights with leveraging the laws of the FDCPA, and the debt collector can levy your assets. That is why it's important to take the necessary steps to avoid being sued. Always use the debt validation strategy to win against debt collectors.

Should consumers fear Debtor Prisons?

It is true that collection agencies are using lawsuits more and more these days, that's why it's important to learn your rights and understand how the FDCPA can help you. One questions consumers asked is, "Can I go to jail for paying my not paying my debts?"

Jump Start Your Credit:
How to Negotiate and Settle your Debts in 10 Steps

In some state of the US there are attorneys who are hired by collection agencies. These attorney know how to use the usury the laws of some states to work in their favor, and consumers have been put in jail because of an outstanding personal debt that is not paid. Whenever cases like this do occur, the debt collector has won a judgment in the court of that state. That is why it is important to know the usury laws of your state. Usury laws are laws that protect consumers from predatory lending of institutions that lend money. These laws regulate how different types of organizations and institutions communicate with consumers along with collection agencies.

If you're wondering how usury laws can help consumers along with it being abused by attorneys to sue consumers, it's because of the loop hole in the law of the state that it's being used. That is why it is so important to answer any legal correspondences that come from the court. If you can show the debt collector that you know your rights, they are more likely to leave you alone. There are many debt collectors that think it is simply too much time and expense for them to take legal action against a debt. Now please I do not want to guarantee you that the collection agency will never sue or try to sue you, but the likely hood could be slim, if you demonstrate to the collection agency that you know your rights. I cannot stress that enough that is why you bought this book. Right????

Should you settle and pay your Debts?

If you have decided that you do not want to leverage the debt validation laws, and you want to go forward with paying your debts. It's important to understand what types of debt are good for settling with a debt collector. A component that must be understood that if you decide to settle on a debt, does not mean that your credit will improve. I cannot legally tell you not to pay your debts, but if you decide to pay them understand paying on your debts will not improve your credit score. I don't care what the debt collector tells you, debt collectors will tell you anything to get you to pay on the debt.

What kind of debts are good candidates for debt settlement:

There are two basic categories of debt, secured and unsecured.

Unsecured debts include:

- medical bills
- credit cards
- department store cards
- personal loans
- student loans
- bounced checks

Secured debts include:

- home
- auto

FYI, you can only settle unsecured debts. Why because with a secured debt, for example a piece of property or automobile, if you stop making payments or default on the loan. The property will be foreclosed on and the automobile will be repossessed.

With unsecured debts, there is nothing "attached" to the loan promised as repayment. Unsecured loans are typically given to people with good or fair credit, due solely to the fact that they have good and fair credit. These are the types of debts that a debt collector is willing to settle, as they have no way to guarantee they will receive anything from you.

How Much Should You Offer to Settle Your Debt?

Jump Start Your Credit:
How to Negotiate and Settle your Debts in 10 Steps

I explained to in the beginning of Part II of this book the difference between the three parties the Original creditor, Collection agency, and Junk debt buyer. And did a further analysis of how the collection agencies and junk debt buyer purchase debts for pennies on the dollar. Now I'm going to give you even a further explanation on how it works and what a collection agency pay.

- Debts that have recently been charged off: 6 to 7 cents on the dollar.
- Accounts that are slightly older: 1.5 cents to 2 cents on the dollar.
- Years-old, out-of-statute debts: A penny or less.

So understand you always want to start your offer at 25% or less. Let me give you an example, if your debt is $1,000 and was recently purchased by a collection agency. That means the collection agency many have paid 7 cents on the dollar, or $70. If you offer them $250 (25%), they are still making a profit of $180. Remember, the credit card companies are out of the picture at this point, so whatever you originally owed the original creditor means SQUAT, why because the money goes directly to the collection agencies.

If you're wondering why start with 25%. because since you know they paid for the debt on a discount why would you offer the full 100%. Starting with 25% can be your starting point, but I would not go beyond 50% of the debt. But keep in mind if the collection agency has not validated the debt, conversations about debt settlement should not be an option; unless you do want to pay.

Should I pay the outstanding balance that is owed?

Jump Start Your Credit:
How to Negotiate and Settle your Debts in 10 Steps

As I mention a few paragraphs previously, I cannot ethically tell you, that if you know the debt is yours and you want to pay the outstanding balance, not to pay it. But if you decide you want to go that route it is necessary that you **PAY FOR A DELETE**. What is "pay for a delete"; it is the process in which you negotiate with the collection agency that if you pay the debt that they will "delete the trade line" off of your credit report. What is "delete the trade line", when you instruct a collection agency to delete the trade line. You're instructing them to delete any derogatory information that is associated on your credit report.

Before you attempt to go forward with this strategy make sure everything you agree on is put in writing and mailed certified receipt. Do not attempt to take the word of someone over the phone with this agreement.

Use this letter to settle an outstanding balance:

AGREEMENT TO COMPROMISE (SETTLE) DEBT

ABC Collections, Inc, referred to as COLLECTION AGENCY and John Q. Consumer, referred to as CONSUMER, agree to resolve the matter of the alleged debt, originally held by the
_____ Company, hereafter referred to as the CLIENT. CONSUMER hereby agrees to settle this alleged debt claimed by COLLECTION AGENCY on the following terms and conditions:

The COLLECTION AGENCY certifies that it is legally authorized to act in behalf of its CLIENT and that any agreement that the COLLECTION AGENCY makes on behalf of CLIENT is legally binding on the CLIENT.

The COLLECTION AGENCY and the CONSUMER agree that alleged debt is $_____.00 (_____ & 00/100 dollars). While the CONSUMER feels that validity of the debt has not been proved by the COLLECTION AGENCY, the parties agree that the COLLECTION AGENCY shall accept the sum of $_____.00 (_____ & no/100 dollars) as full payment on the debt. The acceptance of the payment will serve as a complete discharge of all monies due, and the COLLECTION AGENCY agrees to consider the debt paid in full and agrees to not take further action to collect on the alleged debt. The payment shall be made in the form of a cashier's check or money order.

Upon payment of the $_____.00, the COLLECTION AGENCY agrees to remove any listing or information that the COLLECTION AGENCY may have placed on the CONSUMER'S credit report. The COLLECTION AGENCY agrees to never at any time in the future place any information on the CONSUMER'S credit report.

The CONSUMER feels that the negative information on CONSUMER's credit report is damaging and while the exact estimation of the damage is not currently known, the CONSUMER estimates it to be $10,000 (ten thousand dollars and zero cents). Should the COLLECTION AGENCY fail to remove the listing or reinsert it at a later date, the COLLECTION AGENCY agrees to award liquidated damages of $10,000 to CONSUMER.

This compromise is expressly conditioned upon the payment being received by (date). If the CONSUMER fails to pay the compromised amount by

(date), this contract will be immediately
terminated.

The person signing this agreement,
_____, hereby
declares that he/she is authorized to act as an
agent of the COLLECTION AGENCY.

This Agreement shall be binding upon and inure
to the benefit of the parties, their
successors, and assignees.

Dated:

Signature: _____

Legal Representative of ABC Collections, Inc.

Signature: _____

Jane Doe Consumer

Here are some important Tips When Negotiating Your Debts with Collection Agencies

1. **Its best not talk to a debt collector on the phone.** I cannot stress this enough be very careful, it is best to mail all correspondences and send them certified return receipt. This gives you a paper trail even if you have to go to court.
2. **If you do call them.** Start off the conversation by getting the physical address of the collection agency; you want to know the name of the agency, the direct line and the fax number.
3. **Get your terms *in writing*.** Before you even consider making a payment. Do not accept a verbal offer over the

telephone. Make sure all agreements are in writing and, even then, you will probably have to fight to make the creditor live up to his end of the bargain.

4. **The older the debt, the smaller the settlement**. If the collection agency has called you 50 times and gotten no response, most likely they are going to sell the debt. The debt collector may also choose to sell or assign the debt to a new collection agency *for even less money*, or temporarily ignore the debt.

5. **Don't agree to payments. This is always** a bad idea. If you make payments to a collection agency, little things like extra interest or handling fees could keep your balance from ever going down. In some cases, making a payment restarts the statute of limitations. (I will discuss with you Statue of Limitations later) Wait until you have one lump sum. Remember, the older the collection, the more eager they will be to settle. If they are hounding you, get rid of them by sending a cease and desist letter.

6. **Keep good records.** This can be the difference between a good and bad settlement. Don't expect them to remember you or what you agreed upon.

7. **Send all correspondence via registered mail, receipt requested** This may require a trip to the post office, you be glad you did. Just in case a debt collector tries to sue.

8. **Keep a copy of every letter you send.** Put all correspondence that are type written and mailed out, always make another copy and keep a folder that has all your copies that were mailed.

9. **Keep a log of when you spoke to the agencies, and who you spoke with**. If you decide to talk to a debt collector, make sure you get the name of the Ask for the name of the supervisor of the person you spoke to, as the turnover rate at collections agencies is high.

10. **Follow up all phone correspondence** with a letter (registered, of course).

11. **Penalties and extra interest are typically fictitious amounts of money added on by the collection agency.** Many debt collectors will add as much as much as 50% of the debt or more claimed to be owed by a collection agency consisting of interest and fees. Most companies would be thrilled to get you to pay the original debt even without the extra penalties they add on and will usually be more than agreeable in waiving these fees.

12. **Never look too eager to settle.** Take plenty of time to reach an agreement. Never let it slip that you need to settle the debt because you're buying a home, car or anything else. If you tell a creditor that you really need to get this debt settled to get into your dream home, you can forget any kind of settlement. The creditor will insist on the full balance.

    Try not to accept the first, or even second, settlement offer (unless of course, it's really good). If the collection agency is the one calling YOU to push the deal forward, you have the upper hand. You cannot expect to reach an affordable settlement if the creditor thinks he is in the driver's seat.

13. **Once you hand over the cash, no more time to negotiate.** If you forgot to negotiate the best offer that satisfies your situation. You're out of luck. Make sure you've gone over your agreement with a fine tooth comb, because once a collection agency receive cash from you going back to renegotiate is impossible.

Understand how your credit rating is important in Debt Settlement?

When you are negotiating and settling your debts with a collection agency keep in mind, once it's decided that you will pay the past debt and they will accept your offer. That does not mean your credit score will automatically go up. In order for there to be a change in your credit score, you have to have the trade line deleted. I explained trade lines to you in the in Part I of this book. These are important points to remember when negotiating if you want to improve your credit and increase your credit score.

1. **Collection agencies.** Always insist on a complete removal of a listing from a collection agency. I mean really, who cares if you have a "Paid As Agreed" collection account: no matter what the rating, *every collection account is a negative mark.* It's no skin off their nose to change it, and it offers no use to your credit.

2. **If you do pay the collection agency, you can contact the original creditor and tell them the debt was "settled" and they need to update your account to reflect this.** Technically, they are obligated to do this, as this is the truth, according to the FTC. For the creditor to NOT do this is a violation of the FCRA, because you let them know that this is the law.

3. **In some cases, you can get the collection agency to change your listing with the original creditor.** This really depends and I would not count on it. If the debt was sold to a collection agency then there is no power over what the original creditor will do regarding your credit. To some extent, this is true. However, if the debt has been outsource to a collection agency and not sold then the original creditor want their money. If collection agency gets paid, so does the creditor, therefore it is to their advantage to cooperate.

4. **Remember, though, not all collections result from credit cards.** Doctor's bills cannot appear on your report. But collections resulting from these accounts can. So what that means is that if you went to Dr. John Doe and did not pay the bill. According to HIPPA, that is the regulatory agency that covers patient's rights.

The unpaid doctor bill cannot be put on your credit report, but if the unpaid amount is being handled by a collection agency. They are allowed to have it placed on your credit report, but keep in mind they have to follow the rules of FCRA as well. This is key if the debt is not reflected the right way according to the FCRA it has to remove from your credit report.

If You Have to Accept an Imperfect Credit Listing as Part of Your Settlement

You may find that some of your creditors are willing to hold out longer than you are before agreeing to delete the negative listing from your file. It may seem that they are unwilling to delete the negative listing under any circumstance. That's why it's important to be patient, and be perceived as anxious to have the listing removed.

You can get what you want and the creditor will give in if you speak to the right person, you are patient and persistent, and make the right offer. But if you are on a time-line, and you cannot get them to agree to full deletion, you have this option.

Have the account listed as the following:

List the account as "Paid" only. If the collection agency will not delete the listing have the account listed as "Paid". This is a true indication of the status of the account and many creditors will agree to the wording "Paid". A "Paid" status is still not the best but it is better than having an account that will show "Paid Charge-off" or "Paid Repossession." You should insist that the account show "Paid" *only* and that all other negative notations (such as "Charge-off," "Repossession," late notations, or Collection") are deleted at the same time. A simple "Paid" notation on a regular trade line is neutral and should not hurt your credit.

Jump Start Your Credit:
How to Negotiate and Settle your Debts in 10 Steps

Step 9   Understanding Statues of Limitation

As I mention to you in the previous section, I would discuss Statue of Limitations in-depth further. What is Statue of Limitations and why should I care when it comes to rebuilding my credit. The reason that you the consumer or debtor should care is because collection agencies aka junk buyers have a time period on when they could collect on an outstanding debt. Each state within the US has a time period on when they continue their collection agencies efforts; along with the credit bureaus they have a time line on how long they can list a negative account on your credit report. Listed below are various examples of the different kinds of agreements that a consumer may enter into:

Oral Contract: You agree to pay money loaned to you by someone, but this contract or agreement is verbal (i.e., no written contract, "handshake agreement"). Remember a verbal contract is legal, if tougher to prove in court.

Written Contract: You agree to pay on a loan under the terms written in a document, which you and your debtor have signed.

Promissory Note: You agree to pay on a loan via a written contract, just like the written contract. The big difference between a promissory note and a regular written contract is that the scheduled payments and interest on the loan also is spelled out in the promissory note. A mortgage is an example of a promissory note.

Open-ended Accounts: These are revolving lines of credit with varying balances. The best example is a credit card account. *Please note: a credit card is ALWAYS an open account.* This is established under the Truth-in-Lending Act:

55

Jump Start Your Credit:
How to Negotiate and Settle your Debts in 10 Steps

So now I want to go back to my previous statement, "why should I care about the Statue of Limitations"? The reason why you should care is because many consumers pay off old collection accounts and charge-offs even though the Statute of Limitations has already expired for these accounts. Debt collection accounts that are passed the Statue of Limitations are called "Time Barred Debts", according to the FTC.

Many consumers pay off these "Time Barred Debt" accounts because the accounts still appear on their credit reports or they're being harassed by a collection company. There are state laws that determine how long the Statute of Limitations lasts. Usually, the clock starts ticking when you fail to make a payment; when it stops depends on two things: the type of debt and the law that applies either in the state where you live or the state specified in your credit contract.

For example, the statute of limitations for credit card debt in a few states may be as long as 10 years, but most states impose a period of three to six years. To determine the statute of limitations on different kinds of debts under each state's law, check with a legal aid lawyer, another attorney, or your State Attorney General's Office. If you want to know the laws of your state. Go to your state's Attorney General website or go to http://www.naag.org to find out, what the laws are for collection accounts in your state. It's important that you understand how to use the Statue of Limitation to your defense. Each state has laws on how long a debt collector can collect on an account.

The Statute of Limitations for a debt is different from the reporting period for a debt on your credit report, for example negative information stays on your credit report for seven years. So it's important to understand the difference for reporting information for state law and credit reporting.

Jump Start Your Credit:
How to Negotiate and Settle your Debts in 10 Steps

Once the Statue of Limitations is over for a debt in the state that you live, the debt collector can no longer try to sue you, but you have to answer and respond to a debt collector if they are trying to contact you.

The Statue of Limitation protects you from how long a collection company can collect on a debt or sue you for a debt. Outstanding debt that is older than the Statue of Limitations is called **Zombie Debt,** another word for "Time Barred Debts". (Look for the letter in the Appendix to send to collection agencies that harass for **Zombie Debt,** I also include one at the end of this chapter.

Are you wondering when the Statute of Limitations start?

You might be asking yourself, "It has been such a long time since my "open account" has had any activity. When does the clock start ticking for my Statute of Limitations?

The SOL usually starts:

- The first time you fail to make a payment on your account.
- The credit card company sends you a demand letter for the full amount.
- Or, when the account is listed as charged off by the Original Creditor

Should you pay a Time Barred Debt (Zombie Debt)

If the debt collector, gives you a big discount on the debt or promises to remove the listing from your credit report, should you pay? I don't want to advocate not paying your bills, but if you pay a debt that is pass your state's SOL or the credit reporting SOL you have done what the FTC calls revived the debt to start the Statue of Limitations to begin all over. That means the debt collector can now have the collection account appear on your credit report and if you decide not to pay the company can pursue you in court.

In any case, if the creditor fails to sue you in the time allowed by the applicable statute of limitations, you have an affirmative defense against the creditor's claim which can serve as evidence why they cannot pursue the delinquent debt.

Now you may be asking yourself this question does the Statute of Limitations because your debt to go away after it expires, NO it does not. But a consumer does have a defense if the creditor files suit. The consumer must offer the new evidence to avoid a judgment. The evidence will consist of papers the consumer files to support his claim. If the creditor sues you, and you do not prove to the court that the Statute of Limitations expired, you will have a lost lawsuit and a judgment against you. How do provide evidence to avoid judgment? First know the Statue of Limitations laws in your state and number two know when debt went into collection, and third answer all court documents.

Below is a letter to use for a Time Barred Debt also called Zombie Debt.

(Use this letter to stop any collection letters or harassing calls on Zombie debt (you can also send the Cease and Desist letter)

Zombie Debt Letter

Date

Your Name
Your Address
City, State Zip

Jump Start Your Credit:
How to Negotiate and Settle your Debts in 10 Steps

Collection Agency
Collection Agency Address
City, State Zip

Re: Acct # XXXX-XXXX-XXXX-XXXX

To Whom It May Concern:

I am continually being called on the telephone
by your firm over an alleged (fill in the
amount) debt. According to the information
given to us by your firm, the date of last
activity by the original creditor was (date).
The State of Limitations on this alleged debt,
even should it be ours, is X years in the state
of (your state). Since the debt is out of the
statute of limitations, and you are reporting
this on my credit report, you are conducting
collection activities on zombie debt.

I'm sure you are aware of the provisions in the
Fair Debt Collection Practices Act (FDCPA).
However, I would like to point out that your
firm has violated provisions of the FDCPA by
implying that the legal status of the debt is
collectible by reporting the alleged debt to
the credit bureaus. The exact statute:

[15 USC 1692e]
(2) The false representation of --

(A) the legal status of the alleged debt

and

(B) any services rendered or compensation which
may be lawfully received by any debt collector
for the collection of a debt.

I am also doubtful that you would have adequate documentation to prove in court that you have the right to report this negative information on my credit report, and therefore you are in violation of the Fair Credit Reporting Act as well as the FDCPA. However, I will give you the chance to prove that you are lawfully entitled to report this information by requesting an investigation.

Under the FDCPA I am also invoking my right to ask you to stop contacting me unless you can provide adequate validation of this alleged debt or notification that you are ceasing collections activities.

Please remove this account immediately from my credit report or I will have to take legal remedies which may include lawsuits and notifying our state attorney general's office. In addition, I'm sure your legal staff will agree that non-compliance with this request could put your company in serious legal trouble with the FTC and other state or federal agencies. Under the FCRA and the FDCPA, each violation is subject to a $1,000 fine, payable to me.

Sincerely,

Your Signature

This information can be a powerful weapon in unburdening yourself of old debts, as creditors have a limited time in which to sue you. Remember: the Statute of Limitations begins to run from the day the debt - or payment on an open-ended account - was due. Also, this has nothing to do with how long a negative credit item can remain on your credit report.

How long can items remain reporting your credit report?

- Accurate negative information generally can be reported for seven years,
- Bankruptcy information can be reported for 10 years
- Information concerning a lawsuit or a judgment against you can be reported for seven years or until the statute of limitations runs out, whichever is longer; and
- Default information concerning U.S. Government insured or guaranteed student loans can be reported for seven years after certain guarantor actions.
- Tax liens stay on 7 to 10 years from the date PAID.

Jump Start Your Credit:
How to Negotiate and Settle your Debts in 10 Steps

Step 10 Bankruptcy is it Necessary?

Before I proceed to discuss this chapter regarding bankruptcy, I want to provide you with a disclaimer. This chapter is not to provide you with legal advice, if you feel that you need to file for bankruptcy or see a lawyer, then you should proceed with the process. This chapter is to provide you with options, so you do not have to file for either 7 or 13 bankruptcy. For some individuals a bankruptcy may be a quick solution to a long term problem. Many individuals do not know that by filing for bankruptcy you could be putting your personal and professional life on hold or it can be a fresh start in some instances.

I have worked with people who say filing for bankruptcy is the best thing they did, it allowed them to hit the reset button to start all over again. Although that may sound good to hit the reset button, you are still putting your life on hold. Why, because in some career professions if you ever want to seek a position in financial services or insurance, you will not be able to for at least 10 years.

A bankruptcy remains on your credit report for 10 years or more, regardless if it is discharged. Why would you want to put your life on hold? The methods that I discussed in the previous chapters are supposed to be preventive methods that will allow you to know your rights so you can win against a creditor.

I do not want to give my opinion on if bankruptcy is bad or good, but you should weigh your options, the strategies that I discussed in this book is regarding debt collectors relate to credit card debt. But individuals who are seeking relief from bankruptcy can be experiencing other financial problems for example losing a home or fighting a possible wage garnishment.

So I recommend approaching the need to file bankruptcy with caution and take careful consideration. Understand the differences between the two chapter filings, since the changes to the bankruptcy law changed in 2005, it is more favorable to file for relief under Chapter 13 rather than Chapter 7.

In Chapter 13 if you have a steady income, you could keep your property, such as a mortgaged house or car that you could have lost. Also with Chapter 13, the court approves a repayment plan that allows you to use your future income to pay off your debts during a three-to-five-year period, rather than surrender any property. Once you have made all the payments under the plan, you can receive a discharge of your debts.

With Chapter 7, known as a straight bankruptcy, this involves the sale of all assets that are not exempt. Some examples of exempt property include cars, work-related tools, and basic household furnishings. In some instances your property may be sold by a court-appointed official — a trustee — or turned over to your creditors. Since the development of the new bankruptcy laws in 2005, there is a time period during which you can receive a discharge through Chapter 7. It is now necessary that you wait eight years after receiving a discharge in Chapter 7 before you can file again under that chapter; but with a Chapter 13 the waiting period is much shorter and can be as little as two years between filings.

Although a Chapter 7 & 13 bankruptcy may get rid of your unsecured debts and stop foreclosures, repossessions, garnishments and utility shut-offs, and debt collection activities. These two relief options can provide exemptions that will allow you to keep certain assets, but keep in mind exemption amounts vary by state. For example a personal bankruptcy does not erase child support, alimony, fines, taxes, and some student loan obligations.

Many people who consider bankruptcy are burden with debt, and lack the income to bring these debts up to date. These are the same individuals that feel a bankruptcy will wipe their slate clean. I am not one to point fingers at why someone should file for bankruptcy or not, because I am someone who struggle making ends meet too. The thoughts of bankruptcy was something I was considering as well because I was being harassed by debt collectors, there were judgments place on credit report due to me not answering court notices, but once I started educating myself on how to deal with creditors I ceased my motions to file for bankruptcy.

Everything I discussed in this book are strategies that I have used to rebuild my credit and fight debt collectors back. If you become a student of this information, it could save your life from financial ruins.

Here are 4 strategies you should consider to get your debt under control to avoid bankruptcy:

- Face your reality. Head on!! Take one step at a time, you didn't get in debt overnight so you will NOT get out debt overnight
- Reduce your spending and start to live with a realistic spending plan

- Examine what is your highest and lowest debt obligation, look to possibly change the terms with the creditor. So you can reduce your monthly payment
- Plan your strategy for getting out of debt, how you will do this. Think strategically, if you're scare and uncertain, do some research or hire someone to help you.

Now I have provided you with the necessary arsenal you need to get started rebuilding your credit. At this point you should feel empower knowing now you can get your credit straight and how to deal with debt collectors. In the appendix section I have provided you with 10 credit rebuilding letters for you to use. Good luck on your journey!

Appendix

Credit Disputing Letters

Letter 1

(Use this letter to request the Credit Reporting Agency, to delete a disputed item, after Collection Agency was unsuccessful with validating a debt)

«Your Name»
«Address»
«City», «State» «Zip»

«Collection company»
«Address»
«City», «State» «Zip»

«Date»

RE: Account #_____/ Original Creditor's Name

Dear Sir/Madame:

This is a request for deletion of a disputed item. I have attempted to have this alleged debt verified by the alleged creditor and collection agency to no avail. I am respectfully requesting that Creditor's Name do what is legally mandated by the FCRA and FDCPA, and delete the account listing.

Name of Creditor/Agency, Account #_____

On «date», «collection agency» received a demand for validation from me. Attached is a copy of that letter along with the U.S. Post Office return receipt showing they did indeed receive the request. As of today, date, they have failed to provide any proof or respond in any way.

On «date», I sent a second letter. Again, I have received no response. Attached is a copy of the letter and the U.S. Post Office showing they did receive that letter.

On «date», I sent yet another letter. Again, I received no response. Attached is a copy of that letter as well as a copy of the U.S. Post Office return receipt.

The FDCPA states they must cease collection activity until they have produced verification of the alleged debt if so requested. As per the FTC, this includes reporting to the credit bureaus, which they obviously have done illegally. It is quite evident that no such proof of this alleged debt exists or they would have provided it in the previous 4 months since it was requested.

Also, when an alleged debt is disputed, a notation must be entered on the debtors credit report showing the item is in dispute. Again, this was not done, which is another violation of the FDCPA.

As per the FCRA, if no proof of debt exists, it may not be reported to the credit reporting bureaus. The FCRA also states that the credit reporting agencies must accept written proof from the debtor.

Therefore, I am not asking for an investigation to be done, I am requesting that the entry be deleted in its' entirety as there is no proof of its existence as evidenced by my attached documented proof.

Sincerely,

«Your Name»

Letter 2

(AGREEMENT TO COMPROMISE DEBT – use this letter if you want to settle a debt with a collection agency.)

Your Name»
«Address»
«City», «State» «Zip»

«Collection Company»
«Address»
«City», «State» «Zip»

«Date»

RE: Account #_____/Collection Co Name

Dear Sir/Madam:

CONSUMER (Your name), agree to resolve the matter of the alleged debt, originally held by the Original Creditor, hereafter referred to as your client. CONSUMER hereby agrees to settle this alleged debt claimed by COLLECTION AGENCY on the following terms and conditions:

The COLLECTION AGENCY certifies that it is legally authorized to act in behalf of its CLIENT and that any agreement that the COLLECTION AGENCY makes on behalf of CLIENT is legally binding on the CLIENT.

The COLLECTION AGENCY and the CONSUMER agree that alleged debt is $_____.00 (_____ & 00/100 dollars). While the CONSUMER feels that

validity of the debt has not been proved by the
COLLECTION AGENCY, the parties agree that the
COLLECTION AGENCY shall accept the sum of
$_____.00 (_____ & no/100 dollars) as full
payment on the debt. The acceptance of the payment will
serve as a complete discharge of all monies due, and the
COLLECTION AGENCY agrees to consider the debt paid
in full and agrees to not take further action to collect on the
alleged debt. The payment shall be made in the form of a
cashier's check or money order.

Upon payment of the $_____.00, the COLLECTION
AGENCY agrees to remove any listing or information that
the COLLECTION AGENCY may have placed on the
CONSUMER'S credit report. The COLLECTION
AGENCY agrees to never at any time in the future place
any information on the CONSUMER'S credit report.

The CONSUMER feels that the negative information on
CONSUMER's credit report is damaging and while the
exact estimation of the damage is not currently known, the
CONSUMER estimates it to be $10,000 (ten thousand
dollars and zero cents). Should the COLLECTION
AGENCY fail to remove the listing or reinsert it at a later
date, the COLLECTION AGENCY agrees to award
liquidated damages of $10,000 to CONSUMER.

This compromise is expressly conditioned upon the
payment being received by (date). If the CONSUMER fails
to pay the compromised amount by (date), this contract will
be immediately terminated.

The person signing this agreement,
_____, hereby declares
that he/she is authorized to act as an agent of the
COLLECTION AGENCY.

This Agreement shall be binding upon and inure to the
benefit of the parties, their successors, and assignees.

Dated:

Signature: _____

Legal Representative of Collection Company.

Signature: _____

Letter 3

(Use this letter if a Collection Agency is trying to harass you to pay a debt and they have not validated)

«Your Name»
«Address»
«City», «State» «Zip»

«Collection Company»
«Address»
«City», «State» «Zip»

«Date»

RE: Account Number

Dear Sir or Madam:
I request that you CEASE and DESIST in your efforts to collect on the above referenced account.   It is my personal policy not to deal with collection agencies and I will only deal with the original creditor of this account.

You are hereby instructed to cease collection efforts immediately or face legal sanctions under applicable Federal and State law.

GIVE THIS LETTER THE IMMEDIATE ATTENTION IT DESERVES.

Thank you,

Your Name

Letter 4

(Use this letter if you are disputing an item on your credit report).

«Your Name»
«Address»
«City», «State» «Zip»

«Credit Report Agency Company»
«Address»
«City», «State» «Zip»

«Date»
.

RE: Account Number

Dear Sir or Madam:

This letter is a formal complaint that you are reporting inaccurate and incomplete credit information.

I am distressed that you have included the below information in my credit profile and have failed to maintain reasonable procedures in your operations to assure maximum possible accuracy in the credit reports you publish.

Credit reporting laws ensure that bureaus report only 100% accurate credit information. Every step must be taken to assure the information reported is completely accurate and correct.

The following information therefore needs to be reinvestigated. I respectfully request to be provided proof of this alleged item, specifically the contract, note or other instrument bearing my signature. Failing that, the item must be deleted from the report as soon as possible:

Disputed Item Account #

The listed item is completely inaccurate and incomplete, and is a very serious error in reporting. Please delete this misleading information, and supply a corrected credit profile to all creditors who have received a copy within the last 6 months, or the last 2 years for employment purposes.

Additionally, please provide the name, address, and telephone number of each credit grantor or other subscriber.

Under federal law, you have 30 days to complete your reinvestigation. Be advised that the description of the procedure used to determine the accuracy and completeness of the information is hereby requested as well, to be provided within 15 days of the completion of your reinvestigation.

Sincerely,

Your Name

Letter 5

(Use this letter if the Credit Reporting Agency has not responded to your 1st or 2nd request to dispute a requested item.)

«Your Name»
«Address»
«City», «State» «Zip»

«Credit Report Company»
«Address»
«City», «State» «Zip»

«Date»

RE: Dispute Letter of Date, Follow-up Letter of Date

NOTICE OF INTENT TO FILE COMPLAINT

This letter shall serve as formal Notice of my Intent to file a Complaint with the FTC, due to your blatant disregard of the law.

As indicated by the attached copies of letters and mailing receipts, you have been delivered by registered mail both a dispute letter, dated Date, as well as a follow-up letter, dated Date. As of this moment, you have not done your duty mandated under the law. Your inaction in this matter is inexcusable, and your disregard for the law is contemptible. Rest assured, I will hold you to account.

For the record, the following information is being erroneously included on my credit report, as I have advised you on two separate occasions, more than 75 days and again 40 days ago:

Disputed item

If you do not immediately remove this inaccurate and incomplete information, I will file a formal complaint with the FTC. Furthermore, I intend to seek redress in civil action, for recover of damages, costs, and attorneys fees, should you continue in your deliberate obstruction of the law. For this purpose, I am carefully documenting these events, including the lack of response REQUIRED under law from you.

You are further directed to supply a corrected credit profile to all creditors who have received a copy within the last 6 months, or the last 2 years for employment purposes.

Additionally, please provide the name, address, and telephone number of each credit grantor or other subscriber.

Under federal law, you had 30 days to complete your reinvestigation, yet you have failed to respond. Your continued delays are inexcusable.

Be advised that the description of the procedure used to determine the accuracy and completeness of the information is hereby requested as well, to be provided within 15 days of the completion of your reinvestigation.

Sincerely,

Your Name
SSN# 123-45-6789

Letter 6

(Use this letter when the credit reporting agency has not given you a full credit report, after a dispute.)

«Your Name»
«Address»
«City», «State» «Zip»

«Credit Report Company»
«Address»
«City», «State» «Zip»

«Date»

Dear Sir or Madam:

I recently received a partial notice of results of my dispute without a free updated copy of my credit report.

Per the FCRA section 611

(6) Notice of results of reinvestigation.

(A) In general. A consumer reporting agency shall provide written notice to a consumer of the results of a reinvestigation under this subsection not later than 5 business days after the completion of the reinvestigation, by mail or, if authorized by the consumer for that purpose, by other means available to the agency.

(B) Contents. As part of, or in addition to, the notice under subparagraph (A), a consumer reporting agency shall provide to a consumer in writing before the expiration of the 5-day period referred to in subparagraph (A)

(i) a statement that the reinvestigation is completed;
(ii) a consumer report that is based upon the consumer's file as that file is revised as a result of the reinvestigation;
(iii) a notice that, if requested by the consumer, a description of the procedure used to determine the accuracy and completeness of the information shall be provided to the consumer by the agency, including the business name and address of any furnisher of information contacted in connection with such information and the telephone number of such furnisher, if reasonably available;
(iv) a notice that the consumer has the right to add a statement to the consumer's file disputing the accuracy or completeness of the information; and
(v) a notice that the consumer has the right to request under subsection (d) that the consumer reporting agency furnish notifications under that subsection

Within a month of your inquiry, the credit reporting agency should notify you of the results of its investigation and provide you with a new credit report free of charge. Examine it carefully to ensure that the inaccuracies have been fixed or removed.
Please send a copy of my full updated report upon receipt of this letter.

Sincerely,

Your Name

Letter 7

(Use this letter to dispute an item with the Credit Reporting Agency, when they refuse to delete a trade line off your credit report.)

«Your Name»
«Address»
«City», «State» «Zip»

«Credit Reporting Company»
«Address1»
«City», «State» «Zip»

«Date»

RE: Account #_____/Original Creditor's Name

Dear Sir/Madame:

This is a request for deletion of a disputed item. I have attempted to have this inaccurate and incomplete reporting verified by the furnisher of information to no avail. I am respectfully requesting that (Credit Reporting Agency name), do what is legally mandated by the FCRA and delete the account listing from my consumer file.

Name of Creditor/Agency, Account #_____

On <<date>>, (Credit Reporting Agency name) received a notice of dispute from me resulting in (Credit Reporting Agency name) advising me that the account had been verified.

Knowing that the information could not in fact be verified, I proceeded to dispute the information and request verification directly from the furnisher of information for which the FCRA provides for.

On «date», «original creditor>> received a request for verification from me. Attached is a copy of that letter along with the U.S. Post Office return receipt showing they did indeed receive the request. As of today, <<date>>, they have failed to provide any proof or respond in any way.

On «date», I sent a second letter. Again, I have received no response. Attached is a copy of the letter and the U.S. Post Office showing they did receive that letter.

On «date», I sent yet another letter. Again, I received no response. Attached is a copy of that letter as well as a copy of the U.S. Post Office return receipt.

The FCRA states that information reported must be accurate and complete; updated and verifiable. It also provides a dispute mechanism initiated by the consumer through the consumer reporting agency and through the furnisher of information.

As detailed above, I have disputed the information for the referenced account, with both (CRA name) and the furnisher of information directly. I have exhausted all recourses provided for resolution of erroneous information and still the information remains on my consumer report.

The FCRA provides a cause of action for an individual

consumer as well as penalties and liabilities for both consumer reporting agencies and furnishers of information for non-compliance as violations of its provisions.

It is evident that the information reported cannot be verified and therefore must be deleted as required.

When a debt is disputed under either mechanism, a notation must be entered on the debtor's report showing the item as in dispute. Again, this was not done and is a further violation of the FCRA.

Pursuant to the FCRA, if no proof of debt exists and the information reported is not verifiable, it may not be furnished to the consumer reporting agencies nor reported by them. The FCRA also states that consumer reporting agencies must accept written proof from the debtor.

Therefore, I am not asking for an investigation to be done, I am requesting that the entry be deleted in its' entirety as there is no proof of it's' existence and the information presently reported is not verifiable, as evidenced by my attached documented proof.

Sincerely,

«Your Name»

Letter 8

(Use this letter when the Credit Reporting Agency has not properly verified your disputes.)

«Your Name»
«Address»
«City», «State» «Zip»

«Credit Reporting Company»
«Address»
«City», «State» «Zip»

«Date»

Dear Sir or Madam:

On <date>, I requested to be provided with a description of the specific procedures followed by you, including the name, address and telephone number, of who you contacted in order to verify the information that I had previously disputed on date and that you responded had been verified.

The procedural request was made pursuant to FCRA, Section 611, Procedure in Case of Disputed Accuracy (a)(6) (iii) and was signed as having been received by you via certified mail, return receipt requested, on date.

Pursuant to FCRA, Section 611(a)(7), you are required to provide that description and specific information to me no later than 15 days of my request.

You have failed to provide me with the lawfully requested

description and information within the timeframes specified by the FCRA and obviously must not have received the adequate proof as verification from the creditors that would have allowed you to verify the disputed information.

Therefore, please delete from my consumer file, each of the following trade lines that were the subject of the procedural request:

1.
2.
I am not requesting a reinvestigation; I am requesting deletion of these items, as required by the FCRA.

Please provide me with a new copy of my consumer file, reflecting these deletions, to the above-listed address within the next 15 days.

Thank you in advance for your prompt resolution of this matter.
Sincerely,

Your Name

Letter 9

(Use this letter when you're disputing an item with the Original Creditor.)

«Your Name»
«Address»
«City», «State» «Zip»

«Original Creditor Company»
«Address»
«City», «State» «Zip»

«Date»

RE: Account #_____/Original Creditor's Name

Dear Sir/Madame:

This is a request for deletion of a disputed item. I have attempted to have this alleged debt verified by the alleged creditor and collection agency to no avail. I am respectfully requesting that Original Creditor do what is legally mandated by the FCRA and FDCPA, and delete the account listing.

Name of Creditor/Agency, Account #_____

On «date», «collection agency» received a demand for validation from me. Attached is a copy of that letter along with the U.S. Post Office return receipt showing they did indeed receive the request. As of today,<< Date>>, they have failed to provide any proof or respond in any way.

On «date», I sent a second letter. Again, I have received no response. Attached is a copy of the letter and the U.S. Post Office showing they did receive that letter.

On «date», I sent yet another letter. Again, I received no response. Attached is a copy of that letter as well as a copy of the U.S. Post Office return receipt.

The FDCPA states they must cease collection activity until they have produced verification of the alleged debt if so requested. As per the FTC, this includes reporting to the credit bureaus, which they obviously have done illegally. It is quite evident that no such proof of this alleged debt exists or they would have provided it in the previous 4 months since it was requested.

Also, when an alleged debt is disputed, a notation must be entered on the debtors report showing the item as in dispute. Again, this was not done. Another violation of the FDCPA.

As per the FCRA, if no proof of debt exists, it may not be reported to the credit reporting bureaus. The FCRA also states that the credit reporting agencies must accept written proof from the debtor.

Therefore, I am not asking for an investigation to be done, I am requesting that the entry be deleted in its' entirety as there is no proof of it's' existence as evidenced by my attached documented proof.

Sincerely,
Your Name

Letter 10
(Use this letter when validating an account with a collection agency).

«Your Name»
«Address»
«City», «State» «Zip»

«Collection Company»
«Address1»
«City», «State» «Zip»

Re: Collection Account for *Original Creditor*
Account #: _____
Amount: _____

To Whom It May Concern:

This letter is to inform you that the validity of this debt is disputed. I am not sure of the account number, as I have never heard from you regarding this account. The account number I have is the one listed on my Credit Report – which omits the last few digits.

In the spirit of compromise, I am willing to pay this account *IN FULL (or settlement percentage)* if you agree to immediate deletion of this account from any and all credit reporting agencies (Equifax, Experian and TransUnion). The purpose of this settlement is merely to have this item removed from my credit files. It is not to be construed as an acknowledgment of liability for this debt in any form.

If you agree to the terms and accept this agreement,

certified funds for the settlement amount of dollar amount will be sent to *Collection Agency* in exchange for full deletion of ALL references regarding this account from my credit files and full satisfaction of the debt. As certified funds will be used for payment, there shall be no waiting period regarding the deletion of this account from the credit reporting agencies.

<*Collection Agency*> agrees to delete ALL information regarding this account from the credit reporting agencies WITHIN TEN CALENDAR (10) DAYS following receipt of payment as specified above and will not discuss the terms of this settlement with anyone, excluding your client on this account. If contacted by any third party, including credit-reporting agencies, <*Collection Agency*> will not acknowledge that any settlement offer was made, accepted or executed and will, in fact, deny knowledge of any such account.

If you agree to the above terms, please prepare a letter on your company letterhead explicitly agreeing to the same terms as the above settlement offer and have it signed by an authorized representative of <*Collection Agency*>. It will be implied that this letter shall constitute a legally binding contract, enforceable under the laws of <*my state.*>

Your response must be postmarked no later than 15 days from your receipt of this settlement offer or this offer will be withdrawn and I will request full validation of this alleged debt, as provided for by the Fair Debt Collection Practices Act.

**Jump Start Your Credit:
How to Negotiate and Settle your Debts in 10 Steps**

Please address all correspondence regarding this account to:

Your Name
Your Address
City, State Zip Code

ABOUT THE AUTHOR

Lorillia Brown-Phillips known as the "The Money Mentor" is an author, speaker and financial literacy educator. Lorillia's is passionate about teaching Individuals and Small Business Owners the principles of Personal Finance and how to maximize their financial awareness to build wealth. Lorillia is different from other Personal Finance Experts because she helps individuals examine the WHY behind their money problems. Lorillia has created her trademarked program called Money Life Skills™, it is a step by step process which takes individuals from the fundamentals of finanical literacy to wealth creation. The Money Life Skills™ program has been taught to children, college students and adults.

Lorillia earned her Bachelor's degree in Accounting from Rutgers University; she has served as an Adjunct Accounting Professor teaching Financial Accounting 101 at a local community college in New Jersey. She was a former Financial Advisor and Insurance Producer for seven years.

Lorillia has been a financial contributor to Your Black World has appeared on Washington DC's Radio One 1450 Talk Radio Show, several Blogtalk Radio Podcasts and in Upscale Magazine.

This page has been left blank intentionally.

Made in the USA
Columbia, SC
10 March 2018